More Beautiful
BRAIDS

A Prince Paperback Book

Published by Crown Publishers, Inc., 225 Park Avenue South, New York, New York 10003 and represented in Canada by the Canadian MANDA Group

PRINCE PAPERBACKS and colophon are trademarks of Crown Publishers, Inc.

Manufactured in the United States of America

Created and Produced by James Wagenvoord Studio, Inc.
340 East 66th Street, New York, NY 10021.

Designed and illustrated by Sandra Forrest

Library of Congress Cataloging in Publication Data

Wagenvoord, James.
   More beautiful braids.

     1. Braids (Hairdressing)   I. Coen, Patricia.
II. Title.
TT975.W34 1985   646.7'245   85-449
ISBN 0-517-55795-9

10 9 8 7 6 5 4 3 2

More Beautiful
BRAIDS

by
Patricia Coen
and
James Wagenvoord

Prince Paperbacks
Crown Publishers, Inc.
New York

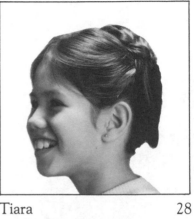

CONTENTS

Before You Braid

Although braids appear to be intricate and complex, braiding is, in fact, a skill that you can easily learn. It just takes a little practice and patience. Once you've mastered a few basic techniques, you'll be able to create both simple and elaborate braids nearly effortlessly. During your first attempts at braiding, you'll begin to sense the rhythms and techniques that make braiding feel natural and comfortable. If your first few attempts at braids are less than perfect, don't be discouraged.

Braiding Basics

Before you begin to braid, it's important to understand the language of braiding—terms used to describe the different techniques and instructions used by braiders.

The **crown** is the topmost part of your head, located by placing the tips of your index fingers above and slightly behind your ears and drawing them upward to meet at the top of your head.

The **hairline** is the line that frames your face (from temple to forehead to temple), where hair begins.

The **nape** is the upper back of your neck hairline.

A **plait** (rhymes with slate) is one complete step in the braiding sequence, i.e., left strand over center strand, right strand over center strand.

Strands are the sections of hair (usually three) that are entwined together to form a braid.

You can make braiding even easier by following a few simple tips:

Lay out the tools you'll need before you begin, so you won't have to go searching for combs, clips, rubber bands, hairpins, or barrettes in the middle of a braid.

Work with damp hair. It holds together easily, leaving fewer stray hairs to worry about.

For your first few attempts at braids, don't try to braid loose hair. Instead, gather your hair into a ponytail anchored by a covered rubber band.

Don't watch yourself in a mirror—the reversed image will only confuse you. Instead, concentrate on what you're doing, closing your eyes if necessary to eliminate distractions. When you've finished, check the results in a mirror. Don't be discouraged if there are stray hairs. After you've braided a few times, you'll be able to feel when there are hairs out of place and gather them into the braid before you finish it.

Visualization is the key to successful braiding. Before you attempt even one plait, imagine yourself carrying out each step on your hair. Braid your hair at first in your imagination, picturing precisely what each step should look like as you do it and when it's completed. This will help you from becoming confused or losing your place as you work.

Relax. People sometimes unconsciously tighten their shoulder muscles as they hold their hands up to braid because the position seems unfamiliar. You'll be more comfortable if you resist this tendency to tighten up.

Maintain equal tension on all the strands of hair as you braid.

Don't worry about taking the "right" amount of hair for each strand. While the strands should be of approximately equal thickness, they needn't be absolutely uniform for the braid to turn out properly.

Enjoy yourself. If you make a mistake, don't worry about it. It will only take a moment for you to unbraid your hair and begin again.

Establishing a Hair-Care Routine

The woven, coiled patterns you create in braiding are enormously enhanced by glossy, manageable hair. Getting your hair in top condition is simple, requiring only a few minutes each day and some common sense. Once you've established a sensible hair-care routine, your braids will always be beautiful.

Everyone's hair is one of three types—dry, normal, or oily—and each type requires slightly different care. For example, daily shampooing may be too drying for hair that tends to be dry, but it won't harm normal hair, and it may be essential to keep oily hair looking clean. Nearly every name-brand shampoo and conditioner is available in three formulas, one for each hair type.

Shampoos & Conditioners

Generally, how often you shampoo depends on your hair type, environment, and activities. Regardless of hair type, you should always shampoo after exposing your hair to chlorinated pool water or salt water, or when you've increased the amount of perspiration present on your scalp by strenuous exercise or by spending time in the sun.

The instructions on most shampoos tell you to lather and rinse your hair twice. Ignore them. One lathering should be enough to clean your hair without stripping its essential natural oils or drying your scalp.

Normal hair can be shampooed daily, although this isn't necessary unless you live in a large city, where dirt and pollution tend to deposit on hair. Use any shampoo formulated for normal hair, with or without a conditioning agent. You may want to use a separate conditioner on normal hair every third or fourth shampoo to keep it at its best.

Oily hair should be shampooed every day, especially in urban areas or humid climates. Use shampoos formulated for oily hair and avoid those that contain conditioning agents, which tend to leave a slightly greasy residue in oily hair.

Dry hair should be washed as infrequently as possible because the detergents and soaps present in all shampoos strip hair of its essential natural oils. Select a shampoo formulated for dry hair, preferably one with a conditioning agent. Special conditioning is necessary to keep dry, flyaway hair under control.

Conditioners make hair shinier, more manageable, and tangle free. Nearly all conditioners contain some form of protein that coats hair shafts to make them thicker and give the hair body. This coating action is more valuable for some hair types than others.

Normal hair and **dry hair** benefit from conditioning. A conditioner will "build up" hair, particularly if it is thin or limp. Dry hair, which tends to be unruly and difficult to manage after shampooing, can be calmed and made shinier by a conditioner.

Oily hair usually gains no benefits from conditioners. Coating the shafts of oily hair sometimes makes it oilier, although some conditioners are formulated especially for oily hair to reduce this tendency.

There are dozens of brands of conditioners. If you use any one brand for more than a month, however, your hair can become immune to its formula, reducing its effectiveness. Each brand combines necessary conditioning agents in different quantities and formulations, and you can avoid building up an immunity to a specific conditioner simply by switching brands. It's best to find three brands that work well for you and use one for a month, then switch to another for the second month and to another for the third. In the fourth month, you can safely return to the first brand.

Grooming & Styling

Treat wet hair gently. Wet hair is weak and can be easily stretched or snapped, resulting in split ends and flyaway hair. Always use a large wide-toothed comb to groom wet hair, as a brush is likely to catch in the hair and snap it.

Although blow dryers are convenient for quick drying, they should be used sparingly. Don't use a blow dryer every day—this will simply dry out your hair too much, even if it's oily. Two or three times a week should be the maximum. To expose your hair to as little potentially damaging heat as possible, let it dry naturally for at least a few minutes before using a blow dryer.

Hair needs to be brushed, but not for the traditional one hundred strokes each day. Twenty-five strokes are sufficient to smooth it and distribute natural oils—any more than that, and you run the risk of damaging the roots.

Braids to Build On

T he illustrations that follow show the creation of the simplest of all braids, the English braid. You can create a single braid at the back of your head by following these instructions exactly; obviously you would place your arms and hands somewhat differently to fashion a braid on the side of your head. You can easily alter the positions shown after you're comfortable with the basics and understand the principles involved in braiding.

There is no single "right" way to braid. Every braider develops individual techniques that are comfortable for her. Our instructions serve as a starting point for beginners and as a reference point/refresher course for experienced braiders.

Every braid is composed of a series of "cross-take-tighten-return" sequences, resulting from motions that flow naturally from and into one another. The sequences are simple—they take longer to describe than to carry out.

Try to create an English braid, copying the illustrated finger and hand positions. It's easy, and you'll quickly begin to adapt the instructions to suit yourself. The key to braiding is what happens to the strands of hair, not the exact finger and hand positions.

The English Braid

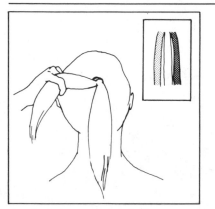

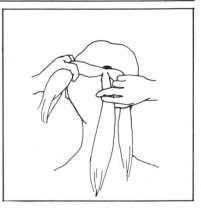

1 Make a ponytail and divide it into three strands. Take the left strand between your thumb and first finger, leaving the other three fingers free.

2 Hold the center strand between your right thumb and first finger and the right strand with your last two fingers, leaving the middle finger free.

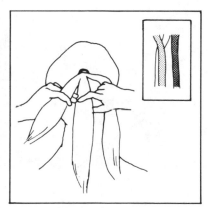

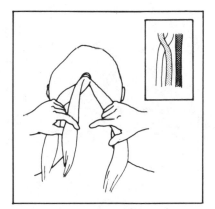

3 **CROSS.** Cross the left strand over the center strand, holding it slightly above the center strand.

4 **TAKE.** Loop the free fingers of your left hand over the center strand and take it from your right hand.

The English Braid

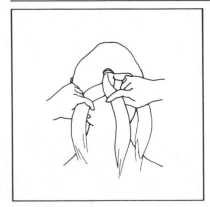

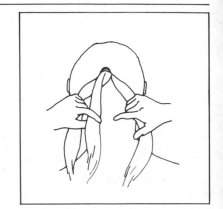

5 **TIGHTEN.** Use your free right thumb and first finger to take the center strand and pull it gently, ensuring that the first half-plait is taut.

6 **RETURN.** Take this new center strand back between the thumb and first finger of your left hand. You're now holding two strands in your left hand and one in your right.

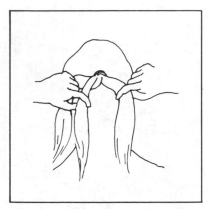

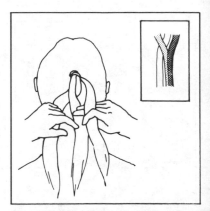

7 Move the right strand so that you're holding it between your right thumb and first finger (if you need to let go of the strand to position it properly, go ahead).

8 **CROSS.** Cross the right strand over the center strand, holding it slightly above the center strand.

The English Braid

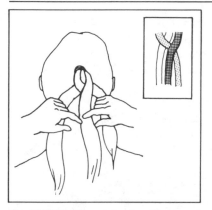

9 TAKE. Loop the free fingers of your right hand over the center strand and take it from your left hand.

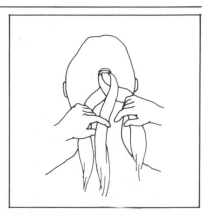

10 TIGHTEN. Use your free left thumb and first finger to take the strand and pull it gently to tighten the plait.

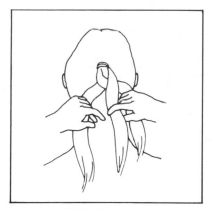

11 RETURN. Take this new center strand back between the thumb and first finger of your right hand. You now have two strands in your right hand and one in your left, held by the last two fingers.

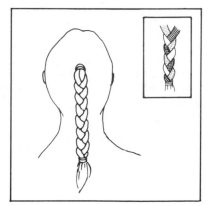

12 Move that strand so that you're holding it between your left thumb and first finger. Go back to step 3 and repeat all the steps until the braid is as long as you want it, then fasten the end with a covered rubber band.

To Free a Hand

As you braid, you'll find that you sometimes need a free hand to smooth the strands you're working with, to gather in stray hairs, or to make sure a plait is positioned properly. At those times, it's easy to hold all three strands in one hand, separated by your fingers. Remember that as you braid, you'll always have two strands in one hand and one in the other. The hand holding a single strand is the one you should free. These illustrations show a braider freeing her left hand while fashioning an English braid.

1   Extend the middle finger of the hand holding two strands.

2   Cross the single strand in the hand to be freed over the center strand. Curl the middle finger around it, holding it between and slightly above the other two strands. You are now holding all three strands in one hand.

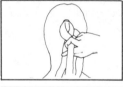

3   To resume braiding, use the last two fingers of the free hand to take the center strand from between the thumb and first finger of your other hand.

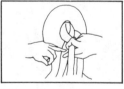

4   Use the thumb and first finger of the hand that you freed to remove the strand held by the middle finger. This makes it the new center strand.

5   You've completed half a plait during these steps. Move the single strand from between the last two fingers to between the thumb and first finger and continue braiding.

Dutch Braids

You've already seen how to create the most basic of all braids, the English braid. By mastering it and two other braids—the Dutch and the French—you'll be able to create any other braided style you like.

But even the simplest English and Dutch braids don't have to be plain. You can decorate them with colorful bows, ribbons, and barrettes, or curl them up into elegant chignons. And an unadorned French braid is one of the most sophisticated of all hair styles. The basics don't have to be boring.

The Dutch Braid is simply the opposite of an English braid. The strands are crossed under, rather than over, the center, so the first plait isn't fitted as closely against the scalp as it would be in an English braid. The finished braid appears slightly flat and loose because the plaits are really upside down. For your first few attempts at the Dutch braid, begin with your hair brushed back into a ponytail with its base slightly below your crown.

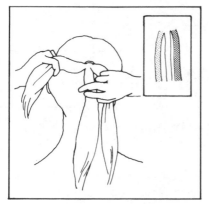

1 Divide the ponytail into three approximately equal strands and position your fingers to begin braiding.

2 Cross the left strand under the center, taking the center strand to the left, so that the two strands trade places.

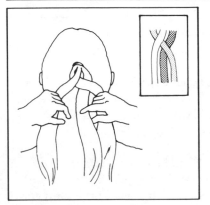

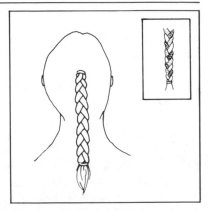

3 Cross the right strand under the center, taking the center strand to the right, so that these two strands trade places.

4 Continue crossing the strands alternately under the center until the braid is as long as you want it, then fasten the end with a covered rubber band.

French Braids

The French braid is deceptively complex in appearance. It is, in fact, simply an English braid with an additional step.

Instead of beginning with three strands that incorporate all your hair, the French braid begins with a thin ponytail skimmed from the top layer of hair. As you braid, you gather additional thin sections of hair and add them to the strands of the ponytail, resulting in gracefully draped hair on either side of the braid. The appearance of the drape varies with the amount of hair you add with each step and the tension you keep on each strand. Experiment to find the look you like best.

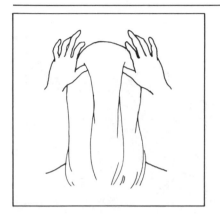

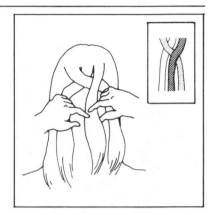

1 Place your thumbs above and slightly behind your ears. Draw them slightly back and upward, gathering hair that meets at your crown into a ponytail. Don't anchor it.

2 Fashion one English plait, crossing the left strand over the center so that the two strands trade places, then the right strand over the center so that those two strands trade places.

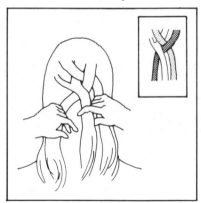

3 Hold the plait in your right hand, separating the three loose strands below it with your fingers. Place your left thumb above and behind your left ear and use it to draw a strand half as thick as one of the original strands toward the ponytail.

4 Add the newly gathered hair to the left strand and cross this increased strand over the center, taking the center strand to the left as in ordinary English braiding.

French Braids

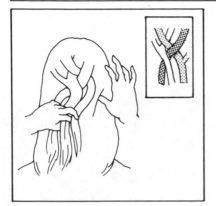

5 Hold the plait in your left hand, separating the three loose strands below it with your fingers. Place your right thumb above and behind your right ear and use it to draw a strand half as thick as one of the original strands toward the ponytail.

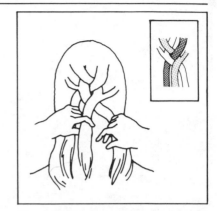

6 Add the newly gathered hair to the right strand and cross this increased strand over the center, taking the center strand to the right as in ordinary English braiding.

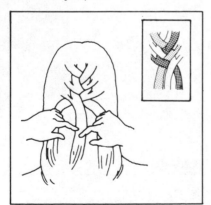

7 Continue gathering hair from the left and right and adding it to the strands just before you cross them over the center.

8 After several plaits, there will be no loose hair left to gather. English-braid the remaining strands and fasten the end of the braid with a covered rubber band.

The Braided Styles

T he styles featured in the following pages are only a few of the
literally dozens of braided looks you can create using the English,
Dutch, and French braiding techniques we've already illustrated. You can
use the step-by-step instructions to braid your own hair or a friend's—in fact,
some of the styles are fairly elaborate and may be easier to fashion on a
friend's hair first, before you try them on your own. These more complex
looks (p. 48, p. 52, and p. 58) are illustrated as if you were braiding someone
else's hair, but the instructions work just as well when you're braiding your
own.

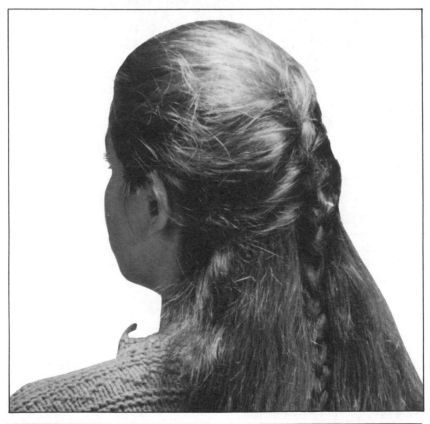

The Cameo

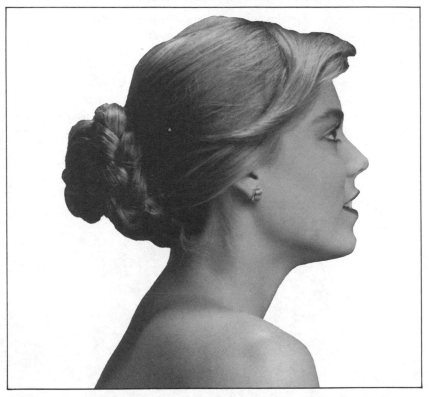

This classic style, often pictured on cameo jewelry, is an appealingly formal look that requires fairly long hair and a bit of patience.

A simple chignon, or bun, is the basis of the Cameo. If you don't have experience in creating a chignon, don't worry. Our illustrations show a braider using a chignon foundation, a doughnut-shaped nylon mesh object available at most notions counters.

You'll gather your hair into a ponytail, draw the ponytail through the hole in the foundation, then spread the strands over the rounded edges of the foundation, pinning them invisibly underneath it to create a perfect chignon. You'll complete the look by English-braiding the loose section of hair at your nape and wrapping it around the chignon.

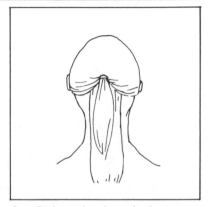

1   Comb your hair straight back from your forehead to eliminate the part.

2   Gather the hair back into a ponytail with its base halfway between crown and nape and anchor it with a covered rubber band. Leave a two-inch-wide section of loose hair hanging below it.

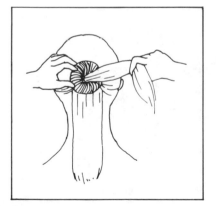

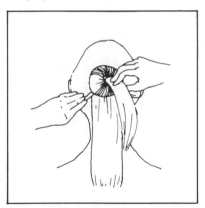

3   Pull the ponytail through the center of the foundation, bringing the foundation up against your head.

4   Take a small section of hair and gently smooth it over the edge of the foundation. Use a hairpin to fasten it underneath.

The Cameo

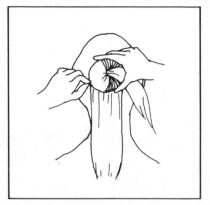

5 Take another small section next to the first one and gently smooth it over the edge of the foundation, using a hairpin to fasten it underneath.

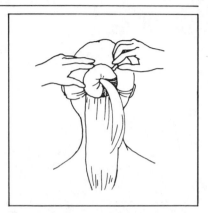

6 Continue smoothing small sections of hair over the edge of the foundation, carefully concealing their ends underneath and fastening them with hairpins.

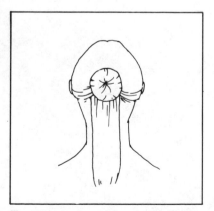

7 When the ponytail has been tucked around the foundation, you should have a neat chignon with a section of loose hair hanging below it.

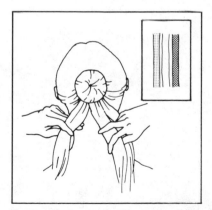

8 Divide the loose section into three approximately equal strands and position your fingers to begin braiding.

The Cameo

9 Cross the left strand over the center, taking the center strand to the left, so that the two strands trade places.

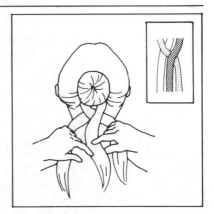

10 Cross the right strand over the center, taking the center strand to the right, so that these two strands trade places.

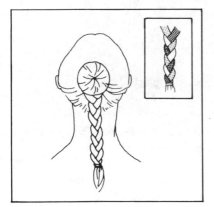

11 Continue English-braiding. When you reach the bottom of the strands, fasten them with a covered rubber band.

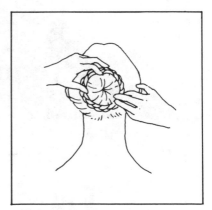

12 Bring the braid up and around the chignon, encircling its base. Tuck the end of the braid under the bottom of the chignon and secure it firmly in place with hairpins.

Ribbon Braid

T his easy-to-make braid is surprisingly versatile and festive. The look varies with the color of the accent you choose to weave in with the English braids.

Make sure that the ribbon or yarn you're weaving in with the braids is at least two or three inches longer than your hair, so there'll be some left over to conceal the rubber band that fastens the braid. Don't worry if the ribbon is too long—you can always trim the ends when you've finished braiding.

You needn't anchor the ribbon in place. When the braid is fashioned properly, it's very taut and the tension between the strands keeps the ribbon secure.

1 Part your hair from the center of your forehead to the nape. The part must be very straight.

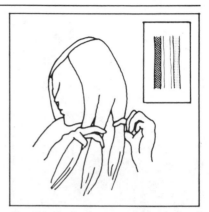

2 Divide the hair on the left side of the part into three approximately equal strands.

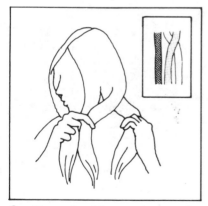

3 Cross the left strand over the center, taking the center strand to the left, so that the two strands trade places.

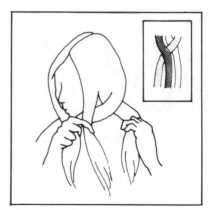

4 Cross the right strand over the center, taking the center strand to the right, so that these two strands trade places.

Ribbon Braid

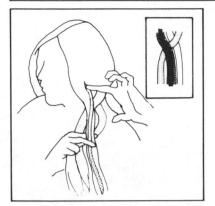

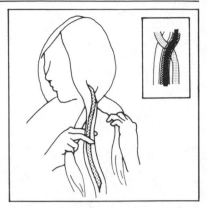

5 Hold all three strands in one hand. With the other, carefully lay the ribbon along the center strand, concealing its end underneath a strand of the plait.

6 The ribbon is now a part of the strand that's currently in the center.

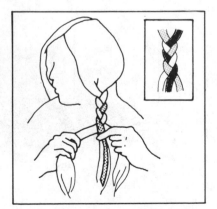

7 Continue regular English-braiding, crossing the left and then the right strands over the center. The ribbon stays with its original strand.

8 When you reach the bottom of the strands, fasten the ends with a covered rubber band. Let the ribbon hang below the strands.

Ribbon Braid

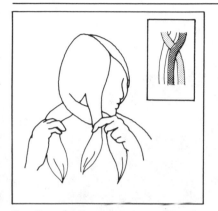

9 Repeat the sequence on the right side. Cross the left and then the right strand over the center.

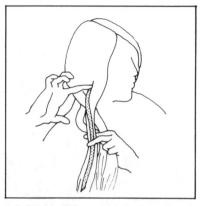

10 Hold all three strands in one hand. With the other, carefully lay the ribbon along the center strand, concealing its end underneath a strand of the plait.

11 Continue English-braiding, keeping the ribbon with its original strand. Fasten the end of the braid with a covered rubber band.

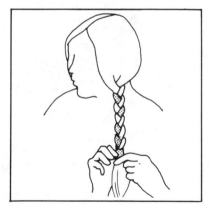

12 Wrap the loose ends of the ribbons around the covered rubber bands. You can secure the ends by tucking them under the wrapped ribbon and into the covered rubber band, or by firmly pressing invisible cellophane tape against the end of the ribbon.

The Tiara

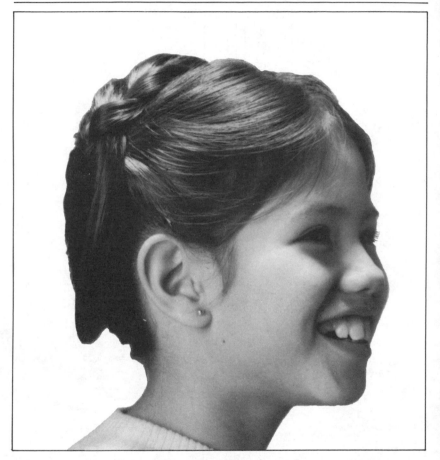

P ractically everybody has, at one time or another, fashioned braided pigtails—one English braid on either side of the head. They're easy to make and perfect for keeping your hair in order and out of your way.

Mothers of little girls especially appreciate the practical and durable characteristics of this look. But, like most braids, these braided pigtails can be more than practical. They can easily be turned into a stylish look simply by using them to encircle the head in a Tiara.

1 Part your hair from the center of your forehead to the nape. The part must be very straight.

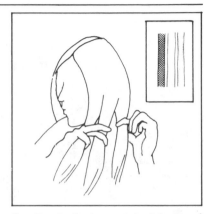

2 Divide the hair on the left side of the part into three approximately equal strands. You can hold the strands taut, so that the braid begins high on your hair, or loosely, so that the braid begins below the ear.

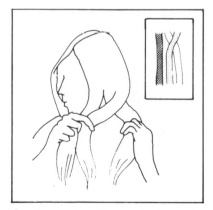

3 Cross the left strand over the center, taking the center strand to the left, so that the two strands trade places.

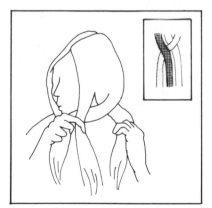

4 Cross the right strand over the center, taking the center strand to the right, so that these two strands trade places.

The Tiara

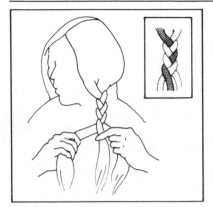

5 Continue English-braiding, crossing the left and then the right strands over the center.

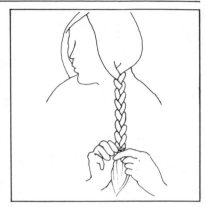

6 When you reach the bottom of the strands, fasten the ends with a covered rubber band.

7 Repeat the sequence on the right side. Cross the left strand over the center, taking the center strand to the left, so that the two strands trade places.

8 Cross the right strand over the center, taking the center strand to the right, so that these two strands trade places.

The Tiara

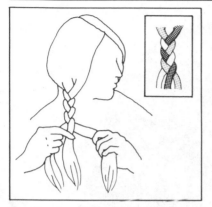

9 Continue English-braiding, crossing the left and then the right strand over the center.

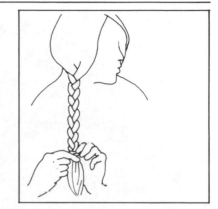

10 When you reach the bottom of the strands, fasten the ends with a covered rubber band.

11 Bring the left braid up and lay it flat against your head with its end pointing toward your right ear. Secure it to the scalp with hairpins.

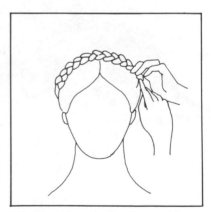

12 Bring the right braid up and lay it flat against your head with its end pointing toward your left ear. Conceal the ends of both braids beneath the plaits and fasten the second braid to your scalp with hairpins.

Duchess Braid

The Duchess braid, a single braid that frames the face, is fashioned using a variation of the French-braiding technique. Ideal for keeping bangs that are growing out neatly away from your face, the Duchess is unusual in that it requires you to begin the braid on one side of your face, gradually braid up toward the top of your head, and then continue down along the other side of your face. Gathering hair from behind the braid and adding it to the strands as you work keeps the finished Duchess braid anchored firmly to the loose hair behind it.

    Although the illustrations show a braider beginning the braid with a one-inch-thick section of hair, you can create a variety of looks with the Duchess braid simply by beginning with different-sized sections of hair.

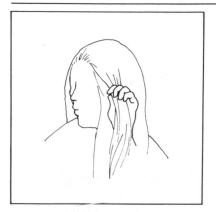

1 Comb your hair straight back from your forehead to eliminate the part, and gather a one-inch-thick section of hair from your hairline just above the temple.

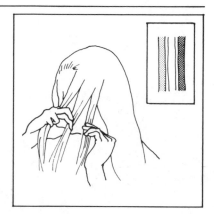

2 Hold this section forward, with its end extending past your face, and divide it into three approximately equal strands.

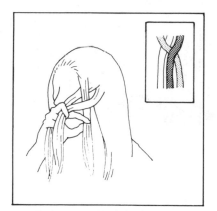

3 Fashion one English plait by crossing the left and the right strand over the center, then hold the plait and loose strands below it with one hand.

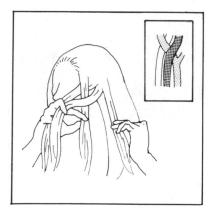

4 Gather a section of hair about as thick as one of the strands from the loose hair directly behind the braid.

Duchess Braid

5 Add the newly gathered hair to the strand farthest from your face, then cross this increased strand over the center.

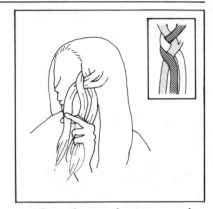

6 Cross the strand nearest your face over the center without gathering any hair, then hold the plaits and loose hair below them in one hand.

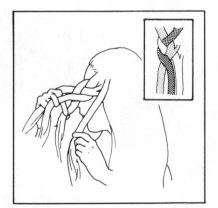

7 Lift the braid slightly toward the top of your head and gather another thin section from the loose hair directly behind it.

8 Add the hair to the strand farthest from your face and cross this increased section over the center strand.

Duchess Braid

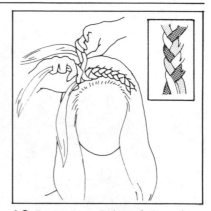

9 Cross the section nearest your face over the center without adding any hair.

10 Repeat steps 7 through 9, working the braid up past the top of your head and down the other side of your face.

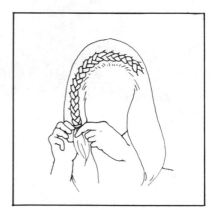

11 When the base of the braid is even with the bottom of your ear, stop gathering hair.

12 English-braid the loose strands and fasten the end with a covered rubber band.

Princess Braid

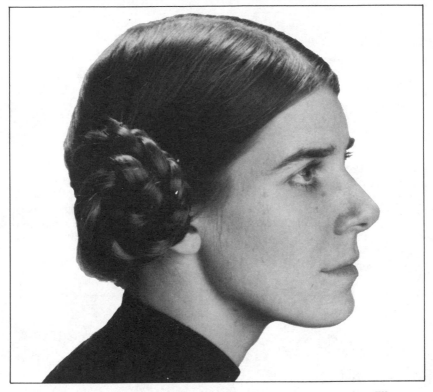

T his look was made famous by Princess Leia in the movie *Star Wars*. In fact, this arrangement of English braids dates back to the fourteenth century, when nearly all women had very long hair and frequently wore braids to keep their hair arranged neatly.

The Princess braid looks good on girls and women of all ages. It works on hair that's slightly above shoulder length or longer. If your hair is at the shorter end of this range, the braided loops you fashion at the sides of your head will be fairly compact. If your hair is very long, you can create longer loops or wrap the braids into two or more loops. The choice is yours.

Our illustrations show a braider beginning on the left side, but you can begin on either side.

1 Part your hair from the center of your forehead to the nape. The part must be very straight.

2 Divide the hair on the left side of the part into three approximately equal strands.

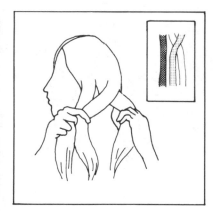

3 Cross the left strand over the center, taking the center strand to the left, so that the two strands trade places.

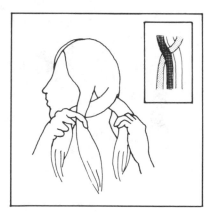

4 Cross the right strand over the center, taking the center strand to the right, so that these two strands trade places.

Princess Braid

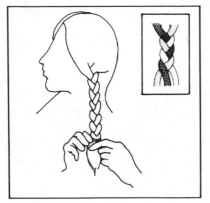

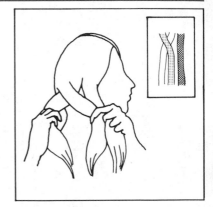

5 Continue English-braiding until you reach the bottom of the strands, then fasten the end with a covered rubber band.

6 Repeat the sequence on the right side. Cross the left strand over the center, taking the center strand to the left.

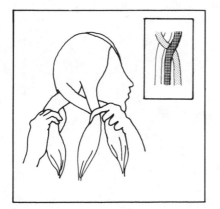

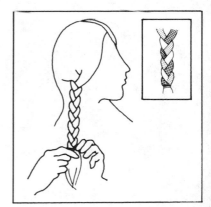

7 Cross the right strand over the center, taking the center strand to the right, so that the two strands trade places.

8 Continue English-braiding until you reach the bottom of the strands, then fasten the end with a covered rubber band.

Princess Braid

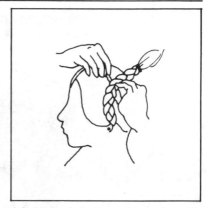

9 Bring the end of the left braid up so that the back of the braid is parallel to your face and curved slightly toward the back of your head. The portion of the braid near the top of your ear will be the midpoint.

10 Use a hairpin to fasten the midpoint of the braid to the hair near the top of your ear.

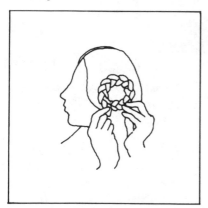

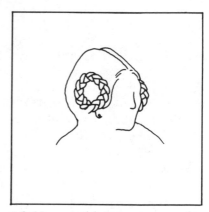

11 Continue curving the braid down around the back of your ear, concealing the braid's end under its base and securing it with a hairpin.

12 Use several hairpins to secure the loop firmly to the hair around it, then repeat on the other side.

Simplified Cornrows

C ornrows are among the most famous of all the braided styles. Like braids themselves, they come in all shapes, sizes, and levels of complexity. Although cornrows were popularized by Bo Derek in the 1979 film *10*, the look is actually a traditional African style that dates at least as far back as the sixteenth century.

A truly expert cornrower can sculpt hair into swirling or symmetrical patterns against the scalp, but even the novice braider can create an intricate cornrow look by fashioning a series of tiny Dutch braids. You can leave the tiny braids hanging loose, but we show them gathered into elaborate pigtails for a more "finished" look. You can also draw the Dutch braids into a thick braided ponytail.

Simplified cornrows can be fashioned from all hair types—straight or curly, thin or coarse. The number of braids you fashion depends on the thickness of your hair and the time you're willing to spend working.

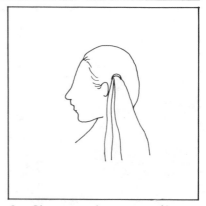

1 Part your hair from the center of your forehead to the nape. The part must be very straight. Gather the hair on each side into a ponytail, with its base anchored firmly against the side of your head.

2 Choose one thin section of hair to braid first. (Decide how many braids you want to create before choosing the width of this section.)

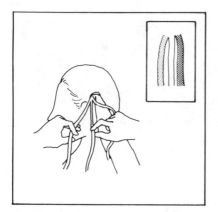

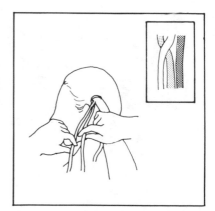

3 Divide the section into three approximately even strands and position your fingers to begin braiding.

4 Cross the left strand under the center strand, pulling them taut, so that the left strand and the center strand trade places.

Simplified Cornrows

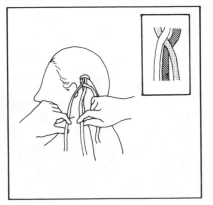

5 Cross the right strand under the center strand, pulling them taut, so that the right strand and the center strand trade places.

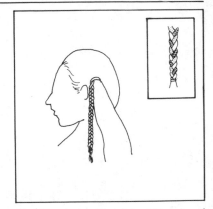

6 Continue Dutch-braiding until you reach the bottom of the strands, then fasten the end with a covered rubber band.

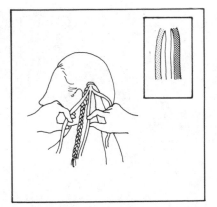

7 Take another section and divide it into three approximately equal strands. Position your fingers to begin braiding.

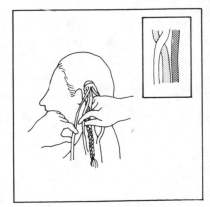

8 Cross the left strand under the center strand, pulling them taut, so that the left strand and the center strand trade places.

Simplified Cornrows

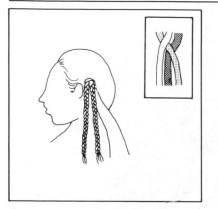

9 Cross the right strand under the center strand, pulling them taut, so that the right strand and the center strand trade places. Repeat steps 6 through 9 until there is no loose hair left.

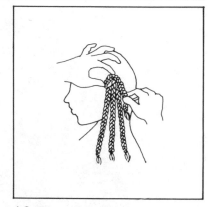

10 When all the hair in one ponytail has been braided, select one braid and wrap it around the covered rubber band that's holding the braids together.

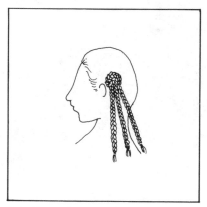

11 Conceal the end of the wrapper braid underneath the covered rubber band.

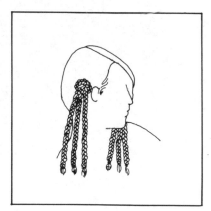

12 Repeat on the other side.

Parisian Braid

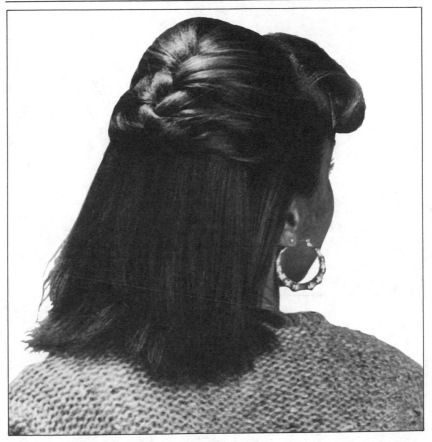

T his pretty and practical accent braid will ornament your hair while
    keeping it drawn neatly back from your face.

You can create the Parisian braid in a variety of sizes. Beginning with a fairly
thick section of hair will give you a wide, sturdy-looking braid; beginning
with a thin section will yield a delicate, slightly wispy-looking braid. Try it
both ways and see which one suits you best.

While using the elegant French braid to create this style gives your
hair a particularly dressy look, English or Dutch braids work just as well.

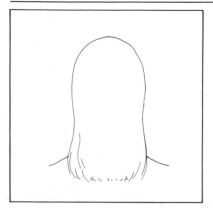

1 Comb your hair straight back from your forehead to eliminate the part.

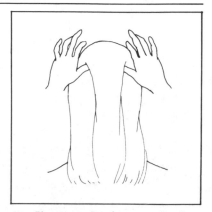

2 Place your thumbs at your hairline, even with your eyes. Draw them back and slightly upward toward your crown, gathering hair as they move.

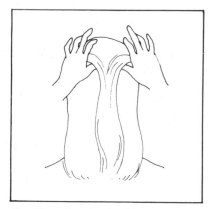

3 Your thumbs should meet at your crown, creating a thin ponytail skimmed from the top layer of hair. Don't anchor it.

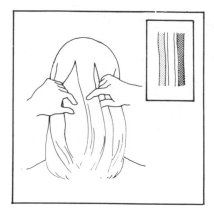

4 Divide this thin ponytail into three approximately equal strands and position your fingers to begin braiding.

Parisian Braid

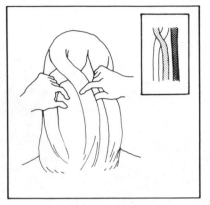

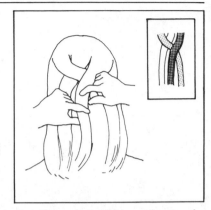

5 Cross the left strand over the center, taking the center strand to the left.

6 Cross the right strand over the center, taking the center strand to the right.

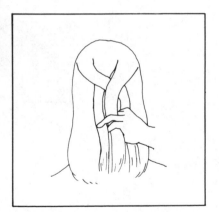

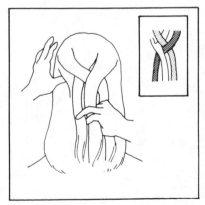

7 Hold the plait in your right hand, its loose strands separated by your fingers.

8 Use your left thumb to gather a very thin strand from the loose hair at the left of the braid. Add it to the left strand and cross this increased strand over the center, taking the center strand to the left.

Parisian Braid

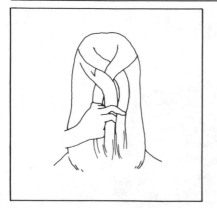

9 Hold the plait in your left hand, its loose strands separated by your fingers.

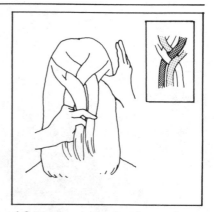

10 Use your right thumb to gather a very thin strand from the loose hair at the right of the braid. Add it to the right strand and cross this increased strand over the center, taking the center strand to the right.

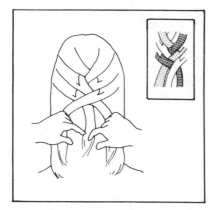

11 Gather hair from the right and left and add it to the strands just before crossing them over the center until the strands are braided halfway down.

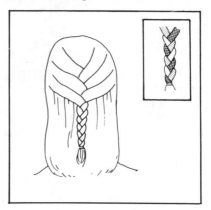

12 English-braid the loose strands until the braid is as long as you want it, then fasten the end with a covered rubber band. You can tuck the hanging portion of the braid up underneath the French plaits and secure it with hairpins.

Gainsborough Braid

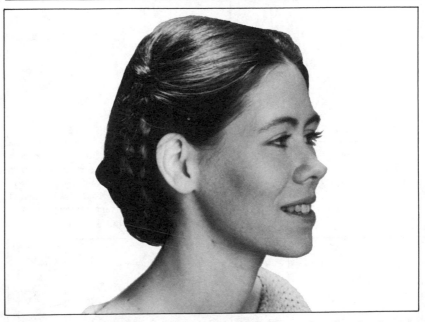

T his nineteenth-century English braid arrangement was considered a suitable daytime style for young women. In the more casual twentieth century, the Gainsborough braid is ideal for special occasions.

Because the style requires that you create and arrange four separate braids, it's best to try it on a friend first. You'll see how simple it really is, and it will be much easier when you try it on yourself.

If you want to try it on your own hair first, remember to visualize each step as you work. As you complete each braid, clip it out of your way so you can fashion the others without becoming confused.

The instructions are written so you can follow them when you're braiding your own hair, and the illustrations show a braider using the instructions on someone else's hair.

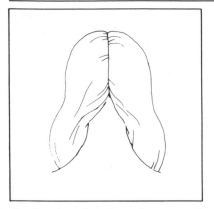

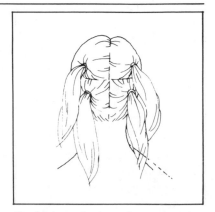

1 Part your hair from the center of your forehead to the nape. The part must be very straight.

2 Make a horizontal part running from ear to ear, so that your hair is divided into four equal sections. Pull each section into a ponytail anchored with a covered rubber band to keep them separate.

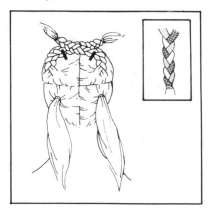

3 Remove the band from the front left ponytail and English-braid only this section of hair, fastening the end of the braid with the covered rubber band. Clip the finished braid out of your way.

4 Remove the band from the front right ponytail and English-braid only this section of hair, fastening the end of the braid with the covered rubber band. Clip the finished braid out of your way.

Gainsborough Braid

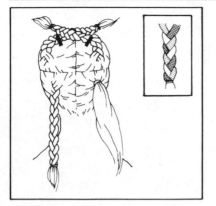

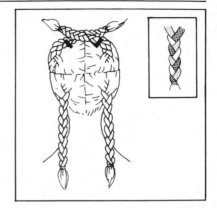

5 Remove the band from the back left ponytail and English-braid this section of hair, fastening the end of the braid with the covered rubber band.

6 Remove the band from the back right ponytail and English-braid this section of hair, fastening the end of the braid with the covered rubber band.

7 Unclip the two front braids, letting all four hang down the back of your head.

8 Bring the back right braid across the nape of your neck, tucking its end under the base of the back left braid. Fasten the end securely to the left braid's base with a hairpin.

Gainsborough Braid

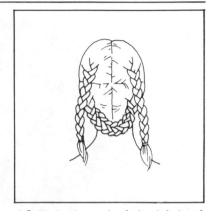

9 Bring the back left braid across the nape of your neck, crossing it over the right braid.

10 Tuck the end of the left braid under the base of the right and fasten it with a hairpin.

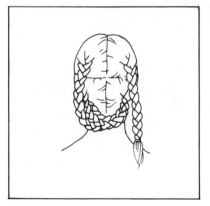

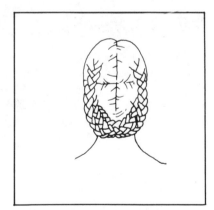

11 Tuck the end of the right front braid underneath the braids at your nape and pin it in place.

12 Tuck the end of the left front braid underneath the braids at your nape and pin it in place.

Evensong

T his stunning style results from combining French and Dutch braiding
techniques to create two braids that stand out from your head.

In the Evensong style, you'll begin by fashioning two Dutch braids,
but you'll also use the French-braiding technique of gathering and adding
hair to strands. Because you'll be crossing these increased strands under,
rather than over, the center strand of each braid, the finished braid will be
elevated from your scalp, with each detail of the braid clearly visible.

The hand motions necessary for creating a Dutch braid while gathering hair into the strands may feel a little awkward, so try it on a friend first
so you can see how it works. Remember, all you really have to do is fashion
two Dutch braids, one at a time, while adding loose hair to the left and
right strands.

The instructions are written so you can follow them when you're braiding your own hair, and the illustrations show a braider using the instructions
on someone else's hair.

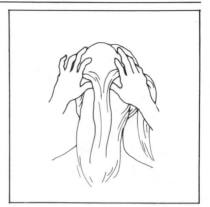

1 Part your hair from the center of your forehead to the nape. The part must be very straight. Gather the hair on one side into a ponytail to keep it out of your way.

2 On the other side, place one thumb against your temple and the other parallel to it at your part. Draw your thumbs toward each other and slightly upward, gathering the top layer of loose hair into a thin ponytail that is the basis of the first Dutch braid.

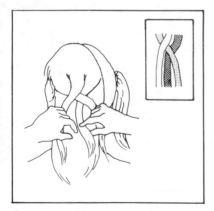

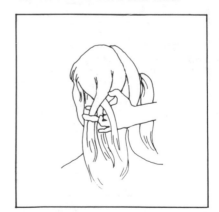

3 Divide the ponytail into three strands and fashion one Dutch plait by crossing the left and then the right strand under the center strand.

4 Hold the plait in your right hand, separating the loose strands below it with your fingers.

Evensong

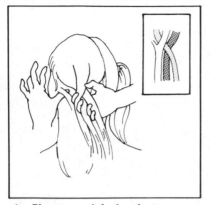

5 Place your left thumb near your face, slightly below the plait. Draw a strand half as thick as one of the original strands toward the plait and add it to the left strand.

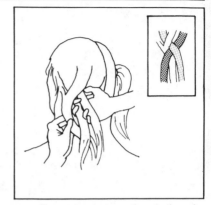

6 Cross this increased strand under the center strand, taking the center strand to the left.

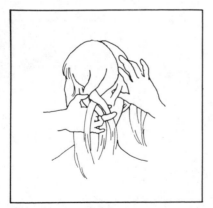

7 Hold the plait in your left hand, separating the loose strands below it with your fingers. Place your right thumb at the part, slightly below the plait.

8 Draw a strand half as thick as one of the original strands toward the plait and add it to the right strand.

Evensong

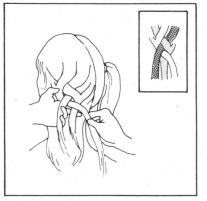

9 Cross this increased strand under the center strand, taking the center strand to the right.

10 Continue gathering hair from the left and right and adding it to the strands just before you cross them under the center. When there is no more hair left to gather, Dutch-braid the strands and fasten the end with a covered rubber band.

11 Unfasten the ponytail on the other side and place one thumb against your temple and the other parallel to it at your part.

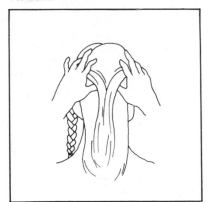

12 Draw your thumbs toward each other and slightly upward, gathering the top layer of loose hair into a thin ponytail, which is the basis of the second Dutch braid.

Evensong

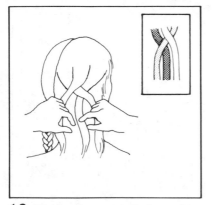

13 Divide the ponytail into three strands and fashion one Dutch plait by crossing the left and then the right strand under the center strand.

14 Hold the plait in your right hand, separating the loose strands below it with your fingers. Place your left thumb at the part, slightly below the plait.

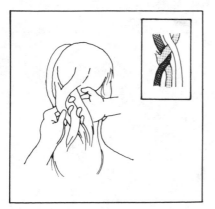

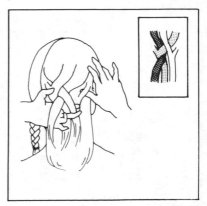

15 Draw a strand half as thick as one of the original strands toward the plait. Add this newly gathered hair to the left strand and cross this increased strand under the center strand, taking the center strand to the left.

16 Hold the plait in your left hand, separating the loose strands below it with your fingers. Place your right thumb near your face, slightly below the plait. Draw a strand half as thick as one of the original strands toward the plait and add it to the right strand.

Evensong

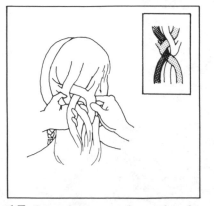

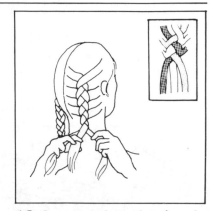

17 Cross this increased strand under the center strand, taking the center strand to the right.

18 Continue gathering hair from the left and right and adding it to the strands just before you cross them under the center.

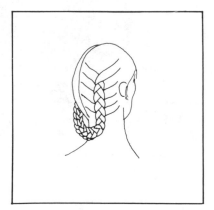

19 When there is no more hair left to gather, Dutch-braid the strands and fasten the end with a covered rubber band.

20 Cross the braids at your nape, fastening each end underneath the opposite braid with a hairpin.

Josephine's Braids

T his sophisticated look is created by partially fashioning one French and one combination French-Dutch braid, one above the other, then combining the loose strands of both braids, English-braiding them together, and coiling them into a chignon.

It's important to position each braid . Remember that you want the finished chignon to be about midway between your crown and nape, so the top braid should begin high up on your head, just below the crown.

The instructions are written so you can follow them when you're braiding your own hair, and the illustrations show a braider using the instructions on someone else's hair.

1   Comb your hair straight back from your forehead and make a horizontal part running from ear to ear, dividing your hair into two equal sections.

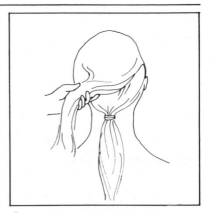

2   You'll work with the top section first, so gather the bottom section into a ponytail and fasten it with a covered rubber band to keep it out of your way.

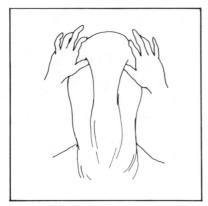

3   Place your thumbs at your hairline, even with your eyes, and draw them up to your crown to create a thin ponytail skimmed from the top layer of hair.

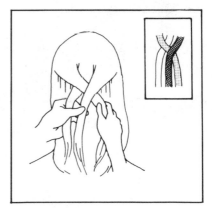

4   Divide this hair into three approximately equal strands and fashion one English plait by taking the left and then the right strand over the center.

Josephine's Braids

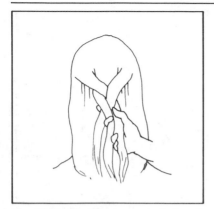

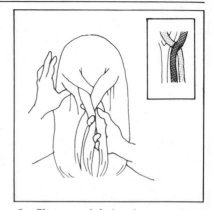

5 Hold the plait in your right hand, separating the loose strands below it with your fingers.

6 Place your left thumb at your hairline, even with the top of your eyebrow. Use it to gather a strand half as thick as one of the original strands from the loose hair and add it to the left strand.

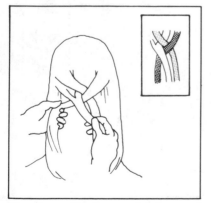

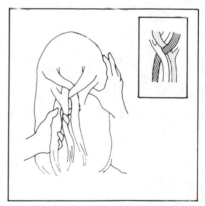

7 Cross this increased left strand over the center, pulling it taut, so that the center strand and the left strand trade places.

8 Place your right thumb at your hairline, even with the top of your eyebrow. Use it to gather a strand half as thick as one of the original strands from the loose hair and add it to the right strand.

Josephine's Braids

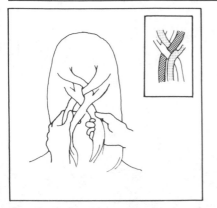

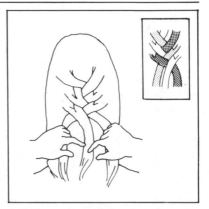

9 Cross this increased right strand over the center, pulling it taut. The center strand and the right strand trade places.

10 Continue gathering hair from the left and right and adding it to the strands just before you cross them over the center.

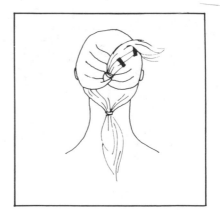

11 When there is no loose hair left to gather, fasten the unbraided strands tightly together with a covered rubber band just below the plaits.

12 Pin the hair up and out of your way. You will use a combination of French and Dutch braiding techniques on the bottom section of hair.

Josephine's Braids

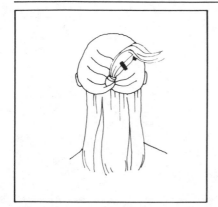

13 Unfasten the bottom ponytail dividing it into three sections. The center section should be about twice as thick as the two other sections.

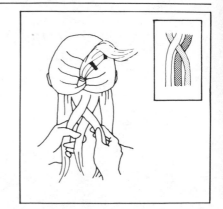

14 Divide the center section into three equal strands and fashion one Dutch plait, crossing the left and then the right strand under the center.

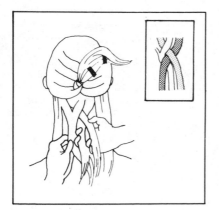

15 Holding the plait in your right hand, gather about a third of the hair from the left section, adding it to the left strand of the center section. Cross this increased left strand under the center strand, taking the center strand to the left.

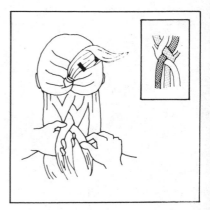

16 Holding the plait in your left hand, gather about a third of the hair from the right section, adding it to the right strand of the center section. Cross this increased right strand under the center strand, taking the center strand to the right.

Josephine's Braids

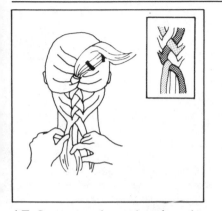

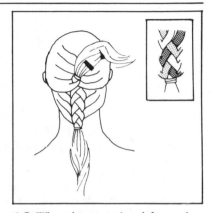

17 Continue gathering hair from the left and right sections and adding it to the left and right strands of the center section before crossing them under the center.

18 When there is no hair left to gather from the side sections, fasten the unbraided strands tightly together with a covered rubber band placed just below the Dutch plaits.

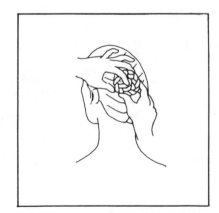

19 Bring the loose hair from the French and Dutch braids together in a ponytail fastened with a covered rubber band. English-braid the ponytail.

20 Place your index finger against your head, touching the base of the braid, and coil the braid around it. Use hairpins to secure the coil tightly to your scalp, concealing the end of the English braid underneath the coil.

About the Authors

Patricia Coen, co-author of *Beautiful Braids* and *The All-In-One Guide to Natural Foods*, has been a contributing writer/editor for nearly a dozen other books including *ComputerSpace, Pasta & Cheese: The Cookbook,* and *ClothesCare.*

James Wagenvoord is a noted author and photographer whose one-man photography shows have been featured in New York and Boston galleries.